# Evensong

# Evensong

## *An Eight-Week Series of Gatherings*

### Volume 2

Barbara Hamilton-Holway

Skinner House Books
Boston

Printed in Canada.

Cover and text design by Suzanne Morgan.
Cover and text illustrations by Patricia Frevert.

ISBN 1-55896-426-6

10 9 8 7 6 5 4 3 2 1
06 05 04 03 02

# Table of Contents

# Introduction

*The most precious gift we can offer others is our presence.*
—Thich Nhat Hahn

Evensong is offered with the belief that these words of the Buddhist monk Thich Nhat Hahn are true. When we offer others the gift of our presence, they open up the truths of their lives to us, and in return we also may speak our own truth. This spirit of mutuality and reciprocity nurtures respect, safety, trust, and mutual regard. Evensong offers participants the chance to share their life experiences, emotions, and doubts with other members of their congregation in an atmosphere of attentive listening without judgment.

At the Unitarian Universalist Church of Berkeley where I serve as co-minister, we start a new Evensong group each month. Many groups continue to meet monthly after the eight sessions. One group has continued now for five years, creating its own topics and orders of service. Other groups have said they wished there were a next series of topics with which they could continue. Some people who have already participated in Evensong may find that this new series of gatherings will help them to get to know a new group of people as well as explore new topics.

To begin your Evensong program, send a letter of invitation to congregation members describing Evensong and providing the details of time and place. The letter should also tell participants how to prepare for the first gathering. (A sample letter is provided on page xiii.) Evensong groups not only meet individuals' needs but they contribute to the whole church community. At the Unitarian Universalist Church of Berkeley, Evensong groups are called on to host work party breakfasts, church luncheons, winter shelter meal preparation, and auction donations. Evensong groups have also participated together in the Gay Pride Parade, the AIDS walk, and the CROP walk. And Evensong is a great way to reach out to newcomers. Try inviting all visitors who sign the guestbook to join the next Evensong group.

Listening is at the heart of Evensong. Listening is a way to show respect and grow in love. Evensong invites people to speak to the depth and essence of their response to questions rather than listing quick responses. The ideal size of a group is eight to twelve participants, small enough so that everyone has the chance to participate equally in the time allotted. Leaders should be people actively involved in the life of the congregation. This will help newcomers feel connected.

## Recommended Setting (for all sessions)

A meeting space where chairs can be set up in a circle around a low table set with a cloth and a chalice (have chalice lit).

## Materials Needed (for all sessions)

- cloth, chalice, and other objects for the table
- *Singing the Living Tradition* for each participant
- the order of service
- quotations cut apart and placed in a bowl or basket (except for the last gathering)
- copies of the preparation pages for the next session.

## Suggestions for Group Leaders

### Beginning

At each gathering, welcome each person and let everyone know you are glad they are there. Begin on time. Let people know you want to honor the time of the gathering—two hours. Some people will have babysitters at home; some have early morning commitments. Arriving on time allows the group to get started and have the time needed to complete the gathering. If time is running out some evening, go beyond the closing time only if all participants agree. Let people know that regular attendance makes for a strong group. Ask people to please notify you in advance if they need to miss a meeting, so you can let the group know.

Begin each gathering by handing out the order of service. Each gathering's order of service is in this book. Worship services can be copied and folded into booklets for participants. Place the first page of the order of service back-to-back with the second page and make double-sided photocopies. Fold the copies in half, forming booklets.

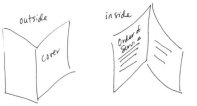

Evensong is shared worship. Each week before you begin, talk through the order of service and invite volunteers to lead parts of the service—speaking the opening, leading the singing, speaking the closing. You can divide the group into two parts for the responsive reading. Opening and closing words and the reminder before sitting in stillness can be said in unison. Everyone has a part in shaping the worth of the gathering. If you would like to end the period of silence portion of the service by ringing a bell, let the group know as you talk them through the service.

*Opening Song*

Music: Genevan Psalter, 1551

OLD HUNDREDTH
L.M. modern form

After the opening words, each order of service includes some lyrics to be sung to the "Old Hundredth," a doxology tune. The tune, provided here, also appears as hymn #371 in *Singing the Living Tradition*.

### Sharing Joys and Sorrows

Each order of service in *Evensong, Volume 2* includes a time for sharing of joys, sorrows, and marking events. Although this sharing is an important aspect of community, it does need to be brief, so it does not take over the time. Not every person needs to speak, although at the first meeting, leaders might ask people during the sharing of joys, sorrows, and marking events to introduce themselves with a sentence or two.

### Holding Each Other in Silent Support

The joys and sorrows do not need to be commented on. The sharing is followed by holding each other in silent support. This silent support may be a minute's pause.

### Reading

Before the gathering, copy the quotations, cut them apart, and place them in a small bowl or basket on the table. Add your own quotations if you like. At the beginning of the reading section, pass the bowl around the circle and invite each person to take a quotation. Continue passing the bowl around the circle until it is empty. When all the readings have been chosen, go around the circle, having people listen to one another read the quotations.

### Sitting in Stillness and Remembering

Giving instructions for the remainder of the gathering before sitting in stillness allows the silence to lead into the sharing. After the reading, remind everyone that the main event of the gathering is the sharing on the evening's topic. People's stories, thoughts, and feelings are personal and sacred, deep material worthy of the group's regard, full respect, and gratitude. Remind the group to save questions or comments for later.

Also, note the time and figure out how much time remains. Remember to allow some time for quiet before the sharing, some time for the group to respond to the sharing, and time for closing. Announce how much time there is for each person to speak. Ask people who want to pass to let the group know so you will know when everyone who wants to speak has done so. You may want to say that the evening's topic is broad and deep, and, of course, none of us will have the time to share all of our thoughts.

Say that members of the group will take turns speaking, not by going around the circle, but by speaking when they are moved to do so. Leaders should speak, too.

Before you begin the sitting in stillness, ask for an individual or a group to volunteer to read the remembering words after the silence. Each night, you might want to introduce the silence with something like, "In the quiet may we get in touch with what we want to say to these people this night."

Have a quiet time of about two minutes. Let the group know in advance how the quiet time will end. You can end the time of silence by ringing a bell or simply by saying, "Let us begin our sharing, showing our care for one another through our attentive listening." After you end the silence, the individual or group will speak the remembering words, which will lead into the communing.

## Communing

Communing is the main event of each meeting. The group responds to each person without comment but with deep listening. During this time, you might model listening by keeping your eyes on the speaker.

If people react to what is said rather than simply allowing each person to speak, you might try just looking down. Most people will remember the plan to keep discussion for later. If a discussion starts, you can politely say that, in order to give everyone a chance to speak, the group will need to hold off on discussion. The time for discussion is after the group has completed the order of service. Then people can linger and talk.

At first, some people may feel awkward not responding when someone speaks, but most people will come to find a time of being held by ears and eyes without comment and debate deeply satisfying.

Sometimes people are listened to so well that they are surprised by what they have to say. If a participant becomes upset, maintain eye contact and try to communicate acceptance nonverbally. If needed, you can say, "That's okay. Take your time." If there are tears, trust that if something needs to be said, you or someone else will find the words and speak. The response might be simply a deep breath and a whispered, "Thank you." There may be a longer silence than usual between that speaker and the next one. You might wait to take your turn at such a moment. Then you can say a little something related to what's just been said before doing your own sharing. Sometimes there may be an awkward silence between speakers or before the first speaker; sometimes the silence may be rich and full, and you may realize how wonderful and how unusual it is to be with a group of people in shared silence.

The Communing might involve a second round in which you can continue the formal structure of each person having a chance to say something he or she had forgotten to say or has been moved to say since their first opportunity. This is still not a discussion, nor time for giving feedback, debating, questioning, advising, or solving. After the communing time, thank everyone for participating, for taking the risk of speaking to people they are only beginning to know. Thank them for sharing something important to them.

Hand out the pages about preparing for the next gathering. Briefly go over the assignment. Invite people to write and/or draw their responses. Stick figures are fine. People may want to try drawing with their nondominant hands. For some, drawing touches deeper emotions than writing. Drawing with the nondominant hand eliminates self-judgment about the drawings.

## Singing and Giving Thanks

After handing out the preparation page, have the group rise as able, to sing a song from *Singing the Living Tradition*. The closing circle follows. People can be invited to join hands and to call out a word or phrase or sentence of gratitude, expressing some appreciation they feel at the moment.

## Closing

Ask the person who volunteered to read the closing words, or the group may read them in unison.

After the close of each gathering, people will probably linger in the room and talk informally. This is often when people will say more to individuals about their sharing by speaking of the connections to their own lives. Relationships and a sense of community are developing and deepening.

Between this gathering and the next send preparation pages for the next gathering to any participants who were unable to attend. After handing out the preparation page, have a volunteer or the group read the closing words. Some groups may be comfortable taking hands for the closing words.

May Evensong be time for personal spiritual development, for a growing willingness to share, and for the gift of a listening presence with one another. Honest, loving speaking and respectful, open listening make community.

# Sample Letter

Evensong
(church)
(address)
(phone)
(fax)

Dear _____ ,

We hope you will be a part of this second series of Evensong. In this Evensong series, participants will explore individual life journeys through sharing thoughts, experiences, doubts, and beliefs. We will meet on (day of week) from (beginning time) to (closing time) at the church.

Again, each week we will follow an order of service with the central event being a sharing time. We will be listening attentively and without interruption to one another. Listening is at the core of Evensong.

Here is our plan:
(date) Gathering 1    Childhood Memory and Knowing
(date) Gathering 2    Scripture and Story
(date) Gathering 3    Prayer and Spiritual Practice
(date) Gathering 4    Fear
(date) Gathering 5    Generosity
(date) Gathering 6    Hospitality and the Stranger
(date) Gathering 7    Being Alive
(date) Gathering 8    Beliefs and Actions

Evensong is a good way to explore personal beliefs and possibilities and a great way to get to know a group of people.

There is no fee for Evensong. To register, please call the church office at (phone).

*For our first gathering, please bring an object, memento, photograph, or drawing that reminds you of a truth you knew as a child that has served you well through life, a truth, a knowing, for which you are grateful. Try to think of a deep understanding or truth you knew as a child, even if your childhood situation was difficult. Was there a strength that, as a child, you found in yourself?*

We look forward to our time together. If you have any questions, please give one of us a call.

Thank you.

_____          _____
(leader's name)                                      (leader's name)


_____          _____
(phone number)                                    (phone number)


_____          _____
(e-mail)                                              (e-mail)

# Leader Preparation

## Gathering One

Create a name tag for each participant and a roster of participants with mailing addresses, phone numbers, and e-mail addresses to distribute to the group

Make sure that everyone who has signed up for Evensong knows to bring an object, memento, photograph, or drawing to share. Invite people to place their items on the table as they speak during the communing. Passing items around distracts people from listening. After the session ends, people can look more closely at the objects. If anyone forgets to bring an object, they can speak to what they would have brought if they had remembered. Usually, the importance of the stories will be more than that of the objects.

## Gathering Eight

Instead of quotations, people may draw each other's names out of the bowl. As people draw out names, they will need to make certain they do not have their own name. Later in the service, after the covenanting, invite each person to speak briefly of what he or she has noticed and appreciated about the person whose name he or she has drawn.

This gathering also includes time for the group to talk about whether they want to continue meeting and whether they want to take on a congregational or community project together.

A response form is also included for people to share their experiences of *Evensong*.

# Gatherings

# EVENSONG

## Gathering One

*Childhood Memory and Knowing*

Opening

We are here to be together,
to celebrate our desire for community,
to grow in respect for self and others.
We worship through our direct speaking
and attentive listening.
Come, let us worship.

Singing

Grace, guide us now as we begin.
Make manifest the love within.
Speak through our lips, hear through our ears.
Touch all our longing, calm our fears.

Sharing Joys
and Sorrows

Holding Each Other
in Silent Support

Responsive Reading

Everyone's story matters.

**The wisdom in the story of the most educated
and powerful person is often not greater than
the wisdom in the story of a child,**

and the life of a child can teach us as much as
the life of a sage.

**Hidden in all stories is the One story.**

The more we listen, the clearer that story
becomes.

**Our true identity, who we are, why we are
here, what sustains us, is in this story.**

In telling stories, we are telling each other the
human story.

**Stories that touch us in this place of common
human-ness awaken us and weave us together
as a family once again.**

—*Rachel Naomi Remen, adapted*

Reading from
the Common Bowl

Sitting in Stillness

Remembering

Perhaps the most important thing we bring to
another person is the silence in us. Not the sort
of silence that is filled with unspoken criticism
or hard withdrawal. The sort of silence that is a
place of refuge, of rest, of acceptance of someone
as they are. We are all hungry for this other
silence. It is hard to find. In its presence we can
remember something beyond the moment, a
strength on which to build a life. Silence is a
place of great power and healing.

—*Rachel Naomi Remen*

Communing

Childhood Memory and Knowing

Singing

"Sleep, My Child"
(Hymn #409 in *Singing the Living Tradition*)

Giving Thanks

Closing

We receive the gifts
of each other's risking and sharing,
the safety and sanctuary
created through our listening presence.
We know moments of kinship,
flashes of insight and spirit.
May the wisdom of childhood
support us now in our living.

## Readings for the Common Bowl

I communed with all that I saw as something not apart from, but inherent in, my own immaterial nature. —*William Wordsworth*

We are all longing to go home to some place we have never been— a place, half-remembered and half-envisioned we can only catch glimpses of from time to time. —*Starhawk*

To that dream-like vividness and splendor which invest objects of sight in childhood, all people, I believe, if they would look back, could bear testimony. —*William Wordsworth*

Childhood is not just a chronological period, a developmental stage to be defined however roughly in years, separating infancy and adolescence, it is an element of the whole person. It may temporarily disappear with the onset of puberty; it may be suppressed, crippled or almost totally atrophied in later life. On the other hand this childhood may continue to grow and develop with life. In childhood we may be wiser than we know. —*Edward Robinson*

The most profound experience of my life came to me when I was very young between four and five years old.
—*respondent to a study by Alister Hardy*

There was a time when meadow, grove, and stream,
The earth, and every common sight,
   To me did seem
   Apparelled in celestial light,
The glory and the freshness of a dream. —*William Wordsworth*

I just know that the whole of my life has been built on the great truth that was revealed to me then (at the age of six).
—*respondent to a study by Alister Hardy*

I believe that many of these childhood experiences are self-authenticating: they bring to the person who has them an awareness of his or her true self as an individual, with an identity, freedom and responsibilities of his or her own. This vision and the experiences which are associated with it are essentially religious.
—*Edward Robinson*

As far back as I can remember I have never had a sense of separation from the spiritual force I now choose to call God.
—*respondent to a study by Alister Hardy*

It was a long time ago. I have almost forgotten my dream. But it was there then, in front of me, bright as a sun—my dream. And then the wall rose, rose slowly, slowly, between me and my dream. Rose slowly, slowly, dimming, hiding, the light of my dream.
—*Langston Hughes*

Know whence you came. If you know whence you came, there is really no limit where you can go. —*James Baldwin*

It is memory that provides the heart with impetus, fuels the brain, and propels the corn plant from seed to fruit. —*Joy Harjo*

How we remember, what we remember, and why we remember form the most personal map of our individuality.
—*Christina Baldwin*

In memory each of us is an artist: each of us creates.

—*Patricia Hampl*

My memory is certainly in my hands. I can remember things only if I have a pencil and I can write with it and I can play with it. I think your hand concentrates for you. I don't know why it should be so.

—*Rebecca West*

Two things are terrible in childhood: helplessness (being in other people's power) and apprehension—the apprehension that something is being concealed from us because it was too bad to be told.

—*Elizabeth Bowen*

I wasn't used to children and they were getting on my nerves. Worse, it appeared that I was a child, too. I hadn't known that before; I thought I was just short.

—*Florence King, on her first day in kindergarten*

I was a very ancient twelve; my views at that age would have done credit to a Civil War veteran. I am much younger now than I was at twelve or anyway, less burdened. The weight of the centuries lies on children, I'm sure of it.

—*Flannery O'Connor*

There is such a rebound from parental influence that it generally seems that the child makes use of the directions given by the parent only to avoid the prescribed path.

—*Margaret Fuller*

Our children are not treated with sufficient respect as human beings, and yet from the moment they are born they have this right to respect. We keep them children for too long, their world separate from the real world of life.

—*Pearl Buck*

A child's attitude toward everything is an artist's attitude.

—*Willa Cather*

All children are artists, and it is an indictment of our culture that so many of them lose their creativity, their unfettered imaginations, as they grow older.

—*Madeleine L'Engle*

Perhaps I may record here my protest against the efforts, so often made, to shield children and young people from all that has to do with death and sorrow, to give them a good time at all hazards on the assumption that the ills of life will come soon enough. Young people themselves often resent this attitude on the part of their elders; they feel set aside and belittled as if they were denied the common human experiences.

—*Jane Addams*

What story (myth, legend, movie, play, fairy tale, Bible story, or scripture from world religions) has really stayed with you?

Write down the story as you remember it.

The Snow Queen - little Gerda was active, not passive
- Cinderella ⎫
- Sleeping Beauty ⎬ passive
- Rapunzel ⎭

the Outlaw Girl was Betty Jo
(rough, mean, but LOVING...
& she gave me things
(warm fur-lined mittens)
Kayuo Masutani → mittens)

The Reindeer - an Animal to carry me away, beyond where I could go by myself ... as I went by Horseback → polo pony

Draw an image or character or event from the story.

What draws you to or away from the story?

To:
- the cold perfect beauty of the Snow Queen
   the ACTIVE nature of the girl
   - her steadfastness - her courage (against frightening things

* Away from: the impersonal evil of the sliver of glass, how a loved one could be transformed... and I could be helpless before this impersonal EVIL that exists ... and can utterly change our situations... and take away that which we loved ──> as with a husband's roving eye and a cold, calculating woman ... who saw advancement, money, travel, status ... and cared absolutely not one iota of the RUIN she brought upon me. I am NOTHING to her... only an obstacle... that she has labelled obsolete.

Looking at the story as a whole, is there movement from one condition to another?

What connections can you see between the story and your life?

What associations do you have with the images and characters and settings of the story?

Where are you in the story—beginning, middle, end?

Now ... I am at the Beginning. But I am not young and fresh, like Gerda, anymore. Where is my Reindeer? Where is the Outlaw Girl, who will arm me and guide me?

I have Courage. I can be Active in my fight. I think I must be all things to myself ... the Reindeer, the Guide.

Is there a way for the transformation in the story to happen in
your own life?

? Possibly, But — does the reward or answer lie in reclaiming Kai. Or ... should I find a truer Kai ... was this Kai (Suhas) never ever what I thought him?

I have been frozen. I am Kai. There is no Gerda to save me ... or must I be my OWN Gerda, reindeer, etc. I think this may be my path — to bring myself back to life. I rejected the passive girls in Cinderella, Sleeping Beauty — I detest the fact that they have to have a Prince ... So maybe I've always known what my life would be.

Time to melt the sliver of icy glass — take it from my eye — get on my reindeer — and Adios! Adios dead love/dead life — Hello warmth, Hello Growth. Hello LIFE. Goodbye Snow Queen/Death.
(Not today.)
(Not yet!)

Try creating a way to honor this story that has stayed significant
to you and pay it tribute for what it has taught you.

**Singing**

"Tallis' Canon"
(Hymn #372 in *Singing the Living Tradition*)
Open our hearts so we may know,
A love that will not let us go,
Alleluia, Alleluia.
A love that holds us from our birth,
A love sustaining all the earth.
Alleluia, Alleluia, Alleluia, Alleluia.

**Giving Thanks**

**Closing**

Life has twists and turns,
is full of heartbreak and joy,
calls forth sacrifice and courage.
No one of us is alone.
We are part of the universal story
in which the spirit breathes.
In us, potential and power abide.
Let us go forth bringing to light the truth of
who we are.

# EVENSONG

*Gathering Two*

*Scripture and Story*

**Opening**

We are here to offer one another our presence,
to bestow the blessing of our listening.
We give each other our trust
as we speak the truths of our lives.
May we hold our time
with one another as sacred.
May we grow in community.

**Singing**

To stories we shall lend an ear,
Extending hands in loving worth;
Our hearts unfold like flowers here,
To fuller life our yes gives birth.

**Sharing Joys
and Sorrows**

**Holding Each Other
in Silent Support**

**Responsive Reading**

The priceless gift of any story lies in its power
to spark a fire in our imagination.

**A great story has the capacity to transcend
the boundaries of our personal worlds, with
their sorrows and joys, and introduce the
universality of human experience.**

Through stories we learn that heartbreak and
joy, grief and love, sacrifice and courage are not
the territory of any time, any culture, nor are
they the blessing or curse of any one individual.

**Stories remind us how timeless and universal
is the search to find peace and freedom, to
live with love and courage, and to be free
from conflict and pain.**

As we are touched by stories, we travel in our
imagination beyond the limits of our individual experience.

**Our hearts are opened to feel the sorrow and
the courage of another person, to experience
the world through the eyes of another, and to
empathize with their struggle.**

As our eyes and hearts open, we begin to see
more clearly our own story reflected in the
stories of others.

**A priceless message of such timeless stories
lies in their capacity to move us to look anew
at our own lives and our own stories.**

Great stories teach us not to despair, not to be
swamped by sorrow or hopelessness; they
remind us in clear and inspiring ways of our
own possibilities and potential.

The stories of others serve as examples and
guides for us, teaching us that the possibility of
great courage, love, and compassion can be
part of our own story.

—*Christina Feldman and Jack Kornfield, adapted*

**Reading from the
Common Bowl**

**Sitting in Stillness**

**Remembering**

Our attentive listening to one another is a way to
show love and create the Beloved Community.

**Communing**

Scripture and Story

## Readings for the Common Bowl

The first and most essential service of a mythology is this one, of opening the mind and heart to the utter wonder of being.

—*Joseph Campbell*

The universe is made of stories, not of atoms. —*Muriel Rukeyser*

There are only two or three human stories, and they go on repeating themselves as fiercely as if they had never happened before.

—*Willa Cather*

The ancient people perceived the world and themselves within that world as part of an ancient continuous story composed of innumerable bundles of other stories.     —*Leslie Marmon Silko*

Fiction reveals truths that reality obscures.     —*Jessamyn West*

We have to make myths of our lives. . . to yield further insight into what it is to be alive, to be a human being, what the hazards are of a fairly usual, everyday kind. . . .     —*May Sarton*

Stories ought not to be just little bits of fantasy that are used to wile away an idle hour; from the beginning of the human race stories have been used—by priests, by bards, by medicine men— as magic instruments of healing, of teaching, as a means of helping people come to terms with the fact that they continually have to face insoluble problems and unbearable realities. —*Joan Aiken*

A lie hides the truth. A story tries to find it.     —*Paula Fox*

There is no agony like bearing an untold story inside you.

—*Zora Neale Hurston*

Page by page, chapter by chapter the story unfolds. Day by day, year by year, your own story unfolds, your life's story. Things happen. People come and go. The scene shifts. Time runs by, runs out. Maybe it is all utterly meaningless. Maybe it is all unutterably meaningful. If you want to know which, pay attention. What it means to be truly human in a world that half the time we are in love with and half the time scares the hell out of us—any fiction that helps us pay attention to that is as far as I am concerned religious fiction.     —*Frederick Buechner*

The tendency of fairy tales is to transform everything internal into something external.     —*Max Luthi*

I am simply trying to conjure up stories in which people are touched with what may or may not be the presence of God in their lives as I believe we all of us are even though we might sooner be shot dead than use that kind of language to describe it.

—*Frederick Buechner*

The fairy tale gives not only pleasure, it gives form and inspiration; and we can readily believe the report of a north German storyteller that a soothing and healing power can emanate from fairy tales when told to sick people in hospitals. Every fairy tale is, in its own way, something of a dragon slayer.     —*Max Luthi*

The best stories are like extended lyrical images of unchanging human predicaments and strong, unchanging hopes and fears, loves and hatreds.     —*Elizabeth Cook*

In some cultures, especially those of the Middle East, stories or fairy tales have several functions. They can both entertain and give pleasure to young children. Often they may contain a useful "moralistic" parable and help to form a common cultural heritage —a shared universe of discourse. They also provide the basis for more advanced instruction later in life.    —*Robert E. Ornstein*

Myth is a large, controlling image that gives philosophical meaning to the facts of ordinary life; that is, it has organizing value for experience.    —*Mark Shorer*

The very essence of myth is that haunting awareness of transcendental forces peering through the cracks of the visible universe.
—*Philip Wheelwright*

We are what we pretend to be, so we must be careful what we pretend to be.    —*Kurt Vonnegut*

It was by speaking God's creative word into the primordial darkness that God on the first day brought forth light, and it is by speaking and listening to each other that out of the darkness of our separate mysteries is brought to light the truth of who we are.    —*Frederick Buechner*

Stories also reveal the powers that provide orientation in people's lives. When people talk about books or movies that touched them, about people they have loved or wanted to emulate, they speak of that elusive sense of meaning, power, and value that roots their mundane stories in something deeper. This depth dimension of stories is crucial, for without it lives would seem empty, meaningless.    —*Carol Christ*

There are works [of art] which wait, and which one does not understand for a long time; the reason is that they bring answers to questions which have not yet been raised; for the question often arrives a terribly long time after the answer.—*Oscar Wilde*

Women's stories have not been told. And without stories there is no articulation of experience. Without stories a woman is lost when she comes to make the important decisions of her life. She does not learn to value her struggles, to celebrate her strengths, to comprehend her pain. Without stories she cannot understand herself. Without stories she is alienated from those deeper experiences of self and world that have been called spiritual or religious. She is closed in silence. The expression of women's spiritual quest is integrally related to the telling of women's stories. If women's stories are not told, the depth of women's souls will not be known.    —*Carol Christ*

Just because it didn't happen doesn't mean it isn't true.
—*Tim O'Brien*

What activity or attitude do you regularly and intentionally engage in that deepens your relationship with the Spirit of Life?

What rituals do you share with others that deepen your relationship with the Spirit of Life?

How has prayer evolved for you from childhood to now?

If you have a home altar or centering place where you place rocks, shells, photographs, candles, art, and/or other objects that you hold dear and that connect you to the sacred, share your altar and your experience of this centering place. If you don't have one, try creating one. What have you chosen to place on your altar? What effect does this space have on you?

In your own language, in your own honest expression, pray what is in your heart.

Try having a regular time throughout the next week for prayer and share your experience with the group.

Create (write, dance, sing, draw, embody . . .) a praise of thanksgiving, a grace before dinner, a reflection acknowledging pain, a greeting for the new day, a healing meditation, a bedtime blessing, a prayer of forgiveness, or whatever is the desire of your heart. If you are willing, share one of your prayers with the group at the next gathering.

# EVENSONG

*Gathering Three*

*Prayer and Spiritual Practice*

| | | | |
|---|---|---|---|
| **Opening** | Spirit of Life,<br>You are the radiance of this moment,<br>Fill our minds with your peace;<br>Fill our hearts with your love. | **Reading from the<br>Common Bowl** | |
| | | **Sitting in Stillness** | |
| **Singing** | Grace, guide us now as we begin,<br>Make manifest the light within.<br>With watchful eye, attentive ear<br>Our thanks for gifts presented here. | **Remembering** | Our attentive listening to one another is a way to show love and create the Beloved Community. |
| | | **Communing** | Spiritual Practice and Prayer |
| **Sharing Joys<br>and Sorrows** | | **Singing** | "The Lone, Wild Bird"<br>(Hymn #15 in *Singing the Living Tradition*) |
| **Holding Each Other<br>in Silent Support** | | **Giving Thanks** | |
| **Responsive Reading** | Prayer is attending to what life gives us and responding honestly, openly. | **Closing** | Let us remember to take a deep breath,<br>to give thanks,<br>offer praise,<br>admit doubts,<br>lament sorrows,<br>voice regrets,<br>speak our hopes,<br>name our intentions.<br>Let us make known the desires of our hearts,<br>and let us listen for what we are called to do. |

**Responsive Reading** (left column continued):

Prayer is attending to what life gives us and responding honestly, openly.

**Prayer is taking a deep breath and slowing down.**

Prayer is listening in the quiet.

**Prayer is hearing the call to a wider perspective, a deeper resolve.**

Prayer is tending the relationship with our truest self or that which is larger than ourselves.

**Prayer is cultivated when practiced every day, regularly, intentionally.**

Prayer is a reminder to live with compassion and care for ourselves, others, and creation.

**Prayer is a rush of thanks for all the gifts of life.**

*Gathering Three*

## Readings for the Common Bowl

Prayers help to quiet and focus the agitated mind. They use words to carry us beyond words. . . By silencing inner noise and distractions, prayer brings us into the presence of the moment.

—*Elizabeth Roberts and Elias Amidon*

Absolutely unmixed attention is prayer. —*Simone Weil*

Three people are stranded on a desert island. Each has a fervent prayer. The first prays to be taken off the island and returned home. The second prays the same. The third prays, "O God, only you know how lonely I am, now that my two friends are no longer here with me. I pray you will return my friends to me on this island."

—*a Sufi story*

I am a humanist who prays, who begins each morning with devotional readings and a time of silence and prayer. Why do I do this? I need a quiet time. I need to express my gratitude. I pray because—alone—I am not enough and also I am too much. I assert my oneness with you and all humankind and all creation.

—*Roger Cowan*

The full autumn moon rises, huge and orange and glowing, and I feel my spirit lifting along with it. "Thank you," I say. "Thank you." In the moment of beauty it doesn't matter whom I am thanking or even whether I am heard. It is enough to be grateful and to be a witness to wonder. —*Lynn Ungar*

Service, especially the prophetic, artistic, dogged work of systematic change for economic justice, is my prayerful response to all I have been given. —*Lucy Hitchcock*

Prayer is an honest expression of how we are in the very depths and doubts of our souls. . . . Prayer is a way of creating a place within ourselves for this Mystery to dwell. Prayer is a covenant we make to be of service. Prayer is a way of living with the very questions that perplex us. —*Daniel Budd*

We can know ourselves and our place in the play of the cosmos through sustained attention to what is going on. I've found the beauty and mystery and grace of our existence are revealed in prayerful attention. Through attention we can come to know the connections. —*James Ishmael Ford*

Those of us who prayed [for a sick friend] found a deeper connection to him, to each other, and to the world we live in—and I know that my friend also found that connection between self and all things. I also know that this connection was more than mere thoughts—it was tangible—as tangible as the medical treatment he also received. —*Nick Page*

I have found my spiritual disciplines—walks in nature, deep conversations, reading ancient and modern scripture, love—or they have found me. —*Dan Harper*

If the only prayer you ever pray is "Thank you," it is enough.

—*Meister Eckhart*

I pray for my daughter, my husband, my mother, and you and for our Fellowship because I know we are linked in ways that are beyond our understanding that quantum physics might begin to explain, that how I hold you in my heart affects you at some level and how you hold me in your heart affects me.

—*Catherine Harris*

Whatever the context or form, prayer is the conscious turning of our attention inward, to lift up for scrutiny that which most concerns us.                                   —*Kathleen McTigue*

The serious part of prayer begins when we have got our begging over with and listen for what I would call the Voice of the Holy Spirit. . . .the Voice I am talking about always says something new and unpredictable —an unexpected demand, obedience to which involves a change of self, however painful.—*Loren Eisley*

Lord, make me holy, but not yet.                        —*Augustine*

Prayer is our tie to the Absolute, a reminder of our nonlocal, unbounded nature, of that part of us that is infinite in space and time and is Divine. It is the Universe's affirmation that we are immortal and eternal, that we are not alone.       —*Larry Dossey*

The prayer of our souls is a petition for persistence; not for the one good deed, or single thought, but deed on deed, and thought on thought, until day calling unto day shall make a life worth living.                                      —*W.E.B. DuBois*

I find that if I'm in a struggle with a person, if I pray for them it changes my relationship to them. I don't know if that's because a transcendent power is intervening or if neural connections in my brain are doing things. But I have to take it seriously, because I've experienced it more and more.          —*Lisa Schwartz*

Pray without ceasing.                            —*Paul of Tarsus*

Prayer is simply being in touch with the most honest, deepest desires of the heart.                          —*Arvid Straube*

In the quietness of this place, surrounded by the all-pervading presence of the Holy, my heart whispers: Keep fresh before me the moments of my High Resolve, that in good times or in tempests, I may not forget that to which my life is committed. Keep fresh before me the moments of my high resolve.
                                         —*Howard Thurman*

Let us be at peace with our bodies and our minds. Let us return to ourselves and become wholly ourselves. Let us be aware of the source of being, common to us all and to all living things. Evoking the presence of the Great Compassion, let us fill our hearts with our own compassion—towards ourselves and towards all living beings.                           —*Thich Nhat Hanh*

Many of us are most familiar with traditional prayers of supplication, in which we ask for favors from a God who seems distant from us. Through life prayer we become co-creators of our world, working in league with a Divine will that is as immediate as our own bodies.              —*Elizabeth Roberts and Elias Amidon*

An everyday spiritual practice is any activity or attitude which you regularly and intentionally engage in with consistency and discipline which significantly deepens the quality of your relationship with the miracle of life both within and beyond you. Everyday spiritual practice is all about living with consciousness, consistency and care that enables you to find right relation, depth relation, caring relation with self, with other human beings, with nature and all its creatures, and with the great mystery of it all (which some call God).                    —*Scott Alexander*

Love is our doctrine, the quest for truth is our sacrament *and service is our prayer.*                 —*Universalist affirmation*

When I was stricken with a mysterious illness . . . I was frightened, too frightened to pray. For the first time in my life, I understood intercessory prayer. I needed the connection, and I was not strong enough or grounded enough to establish it for myself . . . I asked my friend to pray for me . . . I was astonished at its power. I felt the tears, the release, the comfort, and the assurance that the world and all that was sacred would wait for me, would hold a place for me, when I could not do the work of holding it for myself . . . I could feel that the spirit of the universe held me, as it held every living creature. My friend's prayer had touched that spirit as surely as it had mine, and it had done so in my behalf.

—*Anita Farber-Robertson*


Prayer "is an effort to reach deep and to reach out and to become what we would like to be, and need to be, and ought to be. Proper prayer is not a petition to escape realities. It is an effort to face up to realities, to understand them, to deal with them . . . to grow . . . in courage, strength, and in faith. The purpose of prayer is to transform those doing the praying, to lift them out of fear and selfishness into serenity, patience, determination, belonging.

—*Jack Mendelsohn*

Try to remember times when you were first afraid. Where were you?

What happened?

Of what or of whom were you afraid?

Who else was there?

Do you remember sounds, smells, tastes, sights?

How did your body respond to your fear?

What are you most afraid of now?

Try drawing with your nondominant hand a time when you were afraid.

How does your fear paralyze you?

If this fear were lessened, how would you and your life be different?

Jewish and Christian stories are filled with admonitions against fear:

"Fear not, I am your shield."

"Fear not, for I am with you and will bless you."

"Rest assured, do not be afraid."

"Do not fear. I will provide for you."

"Do not fear or be dismayed."

"Be strong and of good courage. I am with you. I will not forsake you."

"Fear not, I will go before you."

"Fear not, peace be to you."

"Fear not, do not let your heart be faint."

"Fear not, I am with you, I will strengthen you, I will help you, I will uphold you."

"Fear not, I have called you by name, you are mine. When you pass through the rivers, they shall not overwhelm you; when you walk through fire, you shall not be consumed."

"You are precious in my eyes, and honored, and I love you."

"Fear not, be glad and rejoice."

"Do not fear. Let not your hands grow weak. I am in your midst. I rejoice over you with gladness. I renew you in my love. I exult over you. I will bring you home."

"My spirit abides among you, fear not."

"Fear not, let your hands be strong."

"Be not afraid; for behold, I bring you good news of a great joy which will come to all people."

"Do not be afraid; take heart."

Try saying words or phrases, singing songs or chants, or whistling tunes that ease your fear and help you find courage or trust within yourself.

**Closing**

Safety is not the most important value.
Let us encourage one another
to live our lives with passion and risk,
to find something important to serve.
Caring makes us vulnerable;
still, let us go toward life
as if our fears had taken a deep breath and
calmed down.
Let us go toward life.

# EVENSONG

*Gathering Four*

*Fear*

**Opening**

There is a love that restores the soul,
a love that makes all things new,
a love that will not ever let us go.
May we trust in that love.
May we rest and be held by that love.
Even when we cannot believe it exists,
love is all around us, among us, inside us.
May love speak through our lips,
Hear through our ears
now and always.

**Singing**

The hurting soul, the weary one
Grace, let a song of comfort come.
Sing to new life the hardened heart.
Calm all our fears and trust impart.

**Sharing Joys
and Sorrows**

**Holding Each Other
in Silent Support**

**Responsive Reading**

Our deepest fear is not that we are inadequate.

**Our deepest fear is that we are powerful
beyond measure.**

It is our light, not our darkness, that most
frightens us.

**We ask ourselves, who am I to be brilliant,
gorgeous, talented, fabulous?**

Actually, who are you not to be?

**You are a child of God.**

Your playing small doesn't serve the world.

**There's nothing enlightened about shrinking
so that other people won't feel insecure
around you.**

We were born to make manifest the glory of
God that is within us.

**It's not just in some of us; it's in everyone.**

And as we let our own light shine, we uncon-
sciously give other people permission to do the
same.

**As we are liberated from our own fear, our
presence automatically liberates others.**

—*Marianne Williamson, adapted*

**Reading from the
Common Bowl**

**Sitting in Stillness**

**Remembering**

Our attentive listening to one another is a way to
show love and create the Beloved Community.

**Communing**

Fear

**Singing**

"Come, Sing a Song with Me"
(Hymn #346 in *Singing the Living Tradition*)

**Giving Thanks**

## Readings for the Common Bowl

I suggested that whenever she felt fear that she think of it as only her first response to whatever was happening. The most familiar response, as it were. I encouraged her to look for and find her second response and follow that. Ask yourself, "If I was not afraid, if I were not allowed to be afraid, how would I respond to what is happening?"
—*Rachel Naomi Remen*

Fear is a question: What are you afraid of, and why? Just as the seed of health is in illness, because illness contains information, our fears are a treasure house of self-knowledge if we explore them.
—*Marilyn Ferguson*

Be not afraid of life. Believe that life is worth living, and your belief will help create the fact.
—*William James*

When fear seizes, change what you are doing. You are doing something wrong.
—*Jean Criaghead George*

To fear is one thing. To let fear grab you by the tail and swing you around is another.
—*Katherine Paterson*

Great self-destruction follows upon unfounded fear.
—*Ursula Le Guin*

What difference do it make if the thing you scared of is real or not?
—*Toni Morrison*

That fear of missing out on things makes you miss out on everything. Keeps you from reality.
—*Etty Hillesum*

I have not ceased being fearful, but I have ceased to let fear control me. I have accepted fear as a part of life, specifically the fear of change, the fear of the unknown, and I have gone ahead despite the pounding in the heart that says: turn back, turn back, you'll die if you venture too far.
—*Erica Jong*

Nothing is so much to be feared as fear. —*Henry David Thoreau*

Grant us wisdom, grant us courage, for the facing of this hour.
—*Harry Emerson Fosdick*

You, the One within all forming in my heart and mind and breath, you, my guide through hate's fierce storming, courage in both life and death, courage in both life and death.
—*Norbert F. Capek*

Empower me to be a bold participant, rather than a timid saint in waiting, in the difficult ordinariness of now.
—*Ted Loder*

If tomorrow morning the sky falls, have clouds for breakfast. If you have butterflies in your stomach, ask them into your heart.
—*Cooper Edens*

I make the effort to see and to passionately open in love to the spirit that infuses all things. I make the effort to see the Beloved in everyone and to serve the Beloved through everyone (including the earth). I often fail in these aspirations because I lose the balance between separateness and unity, get lost in my separateness and feel afraid. But I make the effort.
—*Ram Dass*

Now is the time to commence the litany of hope.
—*Mzwakhe Mbuli*

You promise us new life, and we shrink back from it in fear. Heal us, God, lest we destroy ourselves, We need your presence among us. —*U.N. Environmental Sabbath*

There are only two kinds of people in this world—those who are alive and those who are afraid. —*Rachel Naomi Remen*

Do not be too timid and squeamish about your actions. All life is an experiment. The more experiments you make the better. What if you do fail, and get fairly rolled in the dirt once or twice? Up again you shall never be so afraid of a tumble.
—*Ralph Waldo Emerson*

Fear is that little darkroom where negatives are developed.
—*Michael Pritchard*

To one who is in fear, everything rustles. —*Sophocles*

Our doubts are traitors, and make us lose the good we oft might win by fearing to attempt. —*William Shakespeare*

Do the thing you fear, and the death of fear is certain.
—*Ralph Waldo Emerson*

All through the five acts he played the King as though under momentary apprehension that someone else was about to play the Ace. —*Eugene Field*

Courage is doing what you're afraid to do. There can be no courage unless you're scared. —*Eddie Rickenbacker*

I am tired of being hard, tight, controlled, tensed against the invasion of novelty, armed against tenderness, afraid of softness. I am tired of directing my world, making, doing, shaping. Tension is ecstasy in chains. —*Sam Keen*

Be bold—and mighty forces will come to your aid. —*Basil King*

Courage is mastery of fear—not absence of fear. —*Mark Twain*

Maturity: among other things—not to hide one's strength out of fear and, consequently, live below one's best.
—*Dag Hammarskjöld*

What has been freely, generously given to you?

Do you remember receiving any anonymous gift? What happened and how did you feel?

What story comes to mind of a time when someone gave generously, graciously to you? What happened and how did you feel?

What and from whom else have you learned about giving?

What holds you back in your giving?

Do you have a practice of generosity or can you imagine one? Share your practice or one you imagine.

When have you felt good about giving generously?

Try this before our next session:
Give to someone a loving, anonymous gift with no strings attached.

# EVENSONG

*Gathering Five*

*Generosity*

| | |
|---|---|
| **Opening** | Spirit of Life, You sustain all that is. Fill our minds with your generous understanding. Fill our hearts with your generous love. You support us, now and always. |
| **Singing** | Grace, lead us into our own power. Bless the intention of this hour. Our differing gifts together make Abundance for all to partake. |
| **Sharing Joys and Sorrows** | |
| **Holding Each Other in Silent Support** | |
| **Responsive Reading** | Generous people who love easily,

**who give the benefit of the doubt,**

who willingly offer their gifts and their time and their affection,

**are joyful.**

They are a joy to be around.

**To withhold, to hoard, to grasp, to guard and keep, to hold on tight—each of these is a living death.**

Letting go is relief. Letting go is expansive.

**Giving is freeing. Giving is powerful.**

Not only is it true that as you give, you will be replenished, |

Not only is it true that what you give returns to you,

Giving truly brings you back to life.

**Giving, more generously than you imagined you could, gets the old heart beating.**

Giving makes you feel vital and connected.

**Giving opens you to love of living.**

You are a person who has something to give.

**Live abundantly and delight in giving.**

| | |
|---|---|
| **Reading from the Common Bowl** | |
| **Sitting in Stillness** | |
| **Remembering** | Our attentive listening to one another is a way to show love and create the Beloved Community. |
| **Communing** | Generosity |
| **Singing** | "For the Beauty of the Earth" (Hymn #21 in *Singing the Living Tradition*) |
| **Giving Thanks** | |
| **Closing** | Until we meet again, may power, connection, satisfaction, and joy flow through us in our giving and in our receiving. |

## Readings for the Common Bowl

If you knew, as I do, the power of giving, you would not let a single meal pass without sharing some of it.     —*The Buddha*

You give but little when you give of your possessions.
It is when you give of yourself that you truly give.
—*Kahlil Gibran*

We cannot save our lives. We can, however, spend them for some things that will outlast them.     —*Gordon B. McKeeman*

We Unitarian Universalists often wryly note that we don't offer salvation. But maybe we do, in this transformation of life that happens when you and I navigate that shift from approaching every day asking, "what can I get?" into wondering, "what can I give?" You might even deem it true magic.     —*Margaret Keip*

Wealth is a state of mind. It is actually true that giving generously to others makes us feel more wealthy. It also makes us feel more connected with the life around us.     —*Don Felt*

The older I get, the more I realize that the primary religious quality is generosity: giving liberally of our time, talents, and resources to those communities that bring us abundant life.
—*Tom Owen-Towle*

Money giving is a very good criterion of a person's mental health. Generous people are rarely mentally ill people.
—*Karl Menninger*

If you haven't got charity in your heart, you have the worst kind of heart trouble.     —*Bob Hope*

When we give we feel the depths of our powers—to create, to heal, to love. These are spiritual powers which, when exercised, enlarge our souls. When we give, and when our gift is received. . . both giver and receiver are blessed.     —*Marilyn Sewell*

Small kindnesses make a difference—they have echoes out of proportion to the effort they take.     —*Sue Bender*

If my hands are fully occupied in holding on to something, I can never give nor receive.     —*Dorothee Solle*

How do I thank them, how pay them back? No way, no way at all. You just can't pay. What then? What? Pass it on somehow, he thought, pass it on to someone else. Keep the chain moving. Look around, find someone, and pass it on. That was the only way.
—*Ray Bradbury*

There is only one real deprivation, I decided this morning, and that is not to be able to give one's gifts to those one loves most.
—*May Sarton*

Money is like manure. If you spread it around, it does a lot of good. But if you pile it up in one place, it stinks like hell.
—*Clint Murchison Jr.*

The best way to cheer yourself is to try to cheer somebody else up.     —*Mark Twain*

When I bought my farm, I did not know what a bargain I had in the bluebirds, bobolinks, and thrushes; as little did I know what sublime mornings and sunsets I was buying.

—*Ralph Waldo Emerson*

The fragrance always remains in the hand that gives the rose.

—*Heda Bejar*

Blessed are those who can give without remembering, and take without forgetting.　　　　　　—*Elizabeth Bibesco*

We are rich only through what we give, and poor only through what we refuse.　　　　　　—*Anne-Sophie Swetchine*

How can I believe in God . . . ? I am plagued by doubts. What if everything is an illusion and nothing exists? In that case, I definitely overpaid for my carpet. If only God would give me some clear sign! Like making a large deposit in my name at a Swiss bank.　　　　　　—*Woody Allen*

Many times a day I realize how much my own outer and inner life is built upon the labors of other people, both living and dead, and how earnestly I must exert myself in order to give in return as much as I have received and am still receiving.

—*Albert Schweitzer*

Be kind to all. . . . The best people among you are the ones who are benefactors to others.　　　　　　—*Mohammad*

When you clench your fist, no one can put anything in your hand, nor can your hand pick anything up.　　—*Alex Haley*

All that one gives to others one gives to oneself. If this truth is understood, who will not give to others?

—*Ramana Maharshi*

Don't look for spectacular actions. What is important is the gift of yourselves. It is the degree of love you insert in your deeds.

—*Mother Teresa*

Love has no awareness of merit or demerit; it has no scale by which its portion may be weighed or measured. It does not seek to balance giving and receiving. Love loves; this is its nature.

—*Howard Thurman*

None of us does these things perfectly; that is why we call our efforts "practice." We practice generosity toward others, and we practice it toward ourselves, over and over again. The power of giving grows until it becomes like a great flowing waterfall, until it becomes so natural for us that this is who we are.

—*Sharon Salzberg*

It really is more blessed to give than to receive. Because as you give, you feel powerful and connected and satisfied and joyful. So I ask you: look within and see what you are called upon to give, and give it gladly. If you will but go this way, I give you this promise: you will be blessed as you so give, and you will forget to ask the question, "Do I have enough?" or "Am I strong enough?" Instead, you will find that even as you give, your resources will keep you replenished, and you will feel there is no end to your bounty.　　　　　　—*Marilyn Sewell*

All that you have shall some day be given; Therefore give now, that the sense of giving may be yours and not your inheritor's.

—*Kahlil Gibran*

We are mindful that we shall some day cease our labors, and that others will take up our work—and will build on what we have done. —*Gordon B. McKeeman*

I was learning that what we *bring* to our work, friendships, our family, will directly affect what we get from these relationships . . . That which we withhold is withheld from us; that which we give is given back to us a thousandfold. —*Sue Bender*

Generosity's aim is twofold: we give to free others, and we give to free ourselves. Without both aspects, the experience is incomplete. If we give a gift freely, without attachment to a certain result or expectation of what will come back to us, that exchange celebrates freedom both within ourselves as the giver and in the receiver. In that moment we are not relating to each other in terms of roles or differences; there is no hierarchy. In a moment of pure giving, we really become one. —*Sharon Salzberg*

We went to a lawyer and started the process of making a will. "What would you like to do in case there's an exploding turkey?" asked the lawyer. "What if the whole family was together at Thanksgiving and the turkey exploded? If the four of you were killed at that moment, who would you want to have your worldly goods?" —*Sue Bender*

Please describe or draw some of your personal experiences with both being the stranger, the other, *and* meeting the stranger, the other (class, culture, race, gender, orientation, ability, age, etc.). You might try using your nondominant hand. Do you remember moments of bridging differences, bonding, and religious encounter?

Try reaching out to someone of another class, culture, race, gender, orientation, ability, belief, or age and share your experience with us.

# EVENSONG

*Gathering Six*

*Hospitality and the Stranger*

| | | | |
|---|---|---|---|
| **Opening** | We are all wanderers, passing through, guests of the universe, and our job as a religious clan is to share the earth's bounty and set a warm, inviting place for one another. | | We are called to meet one another face to face, to tell the truth of our lives and to listen! |

—Carolyn and Tom Owen-Towle

—Lee Reid, adapted

**Reading from
the Common Bowl**

**Singing**

Come all in joy now let us sing,
With songs of praise here echoing,
Praise love from whom all blessings flow.
Praise love that with our care can grow.

**Sitting in Stillness**

**Sharing Joys
and Sorrows**

**Remembering**     Our attentive listening to one another is a way to show love and create the Beloved Community.

**Holding Each Other
in Silent Support**

**Communing**     Hospitality and the Stranger

**Singing**     "There Is More Love Somewhere"
(Hymn #95 in *Singing the Living Tradition*)

**Responsive Reading**     We are called forth to join our energies, our talents, our skills, our strength,

**Giving Thanks**

**to join our spirits, our souls in the life work of building the Beloved Community**

**Closing**     Spirit of Life move through us,
calming fears,
bridging distances,
healing wounds.
Spirit of Life move through us,
reaching out,
befriending,
making love and justice.
Spirit of Life move through us,
now and always.

right here,

**right now,**

every day.

**We are called to be chalices,**

flaming chalices burning with passion and compassion,

**chalices wide and deep enough**

to receive the pain and joy of all who hear and feel and respond to our call.

## Readings for the Common Bowl

Hospitality to strangers is greater than reverence for the name of God.
*—Hebrew proverb*

I was a stranger and you took me in.
*—Jesus*

The ritual bond of host and guest contains the consummate religious encounter.
*—Carolyn and Tom Owen-Towle*

The central task of the religious community is to unveil the bonds that bind each to all. There is a connectedness, a relationship discovered amid the particulars of our own lives and the lives of others. Once felt, it inspires us to act for justice.
*—Mark Morrison-Reed*

We are caught in an inescapable network of mutuality, tied in a single garment of destiny.
*—Martin Luther King Jr.*

Remember that you are all people and that all people are you.
*—Joy Harjo*

We are all bound up together in one great bundle of humanity, and society cannot trample on the weakest and feeblest of its members without receiving the curse in its own soul.
*—Frances Ellen Watkins Harper*

As religious liberals, our particular vocation is to provide hospitality for the human spirit in a way that is open and gracious, that gives room both for the realities of human life and the mysteries of God.
*—Rebecca Parker*

Joy will not be complete until all who have received life. . .have returned home and gather together around the table prepared for them.
*—Henri J.M. Nouwen*

The most precious gift we can offer others is our presence.
*—Thich Nhat Hahn*

By working in this moment, for the sake of the land and the people to be in vital relation with each other, we will have life, and it will continue.
*—Simon Ortiz*

If you have been thinking of joining the church, that would be a very significant affirmation. A Big Yes. You will be saying, Yes to playing a part in building a refuge and home for the spirit. You will be saying, "Yes, I want to give myself to that."
*—John Wolf*

May all beings regard me with the eye of a friend, and I all beings! With the eye of a friend may each single being regard all others.
*—Yojht Veda*

There is no break between yesterday and today mother and son air and earth all are part of the other like with this typewriter I am connected with these words and these words with this paper and this paper with you.
*—Norma Jordan*

None of us acting alone can achieve success.
We must therefore act together as a united people.
*—Nelson Mandela*

We are part of a web of life that makes us one with all humanity, one with all the universe.
*—Frederick E. Gillis*

There is a great difference between defending life and befriending it. Defending life is often about holding on to whatever you have at all cost. Befriending life may be about strengthening and supporting life's movement toward its own wholeness. It may require us to take great risks, to let go, over and over again, until we finally surrender to life's own dream of itself.

—*Rachel Naomi Remen*

From the fragmented world of our everyday lives we gather together in search of wholeness. By many cares and preoccupations, by diverse and selfish aims are we separated from one another and divided within ourselves. Yet we know that no branch is utterly severed from the Tree of Life that sustains us all. We cherish our oneness with those around us and the countless generations that have gone before us.       —*Phillip Hewett*

If, recognizing the interdependence of all life, we strive to build community, the strength we gather will be our salvation.

—*Marjorie Bowens-Wheatley*

This we know. All things are connected like the blood which unites one family.                    —*Chief Noah Sealth*

All people are members of the same body, created from one essence. If fate brings suffering to one member, the others cannot stay at rest.                                —*Saadi*

Draw some of your experiences of being alive. You might try using your nondominant hand.

Huston Smith has spoken of what is important from epiphanies or theophanies or ecstatic experiences and it is not the *states* of experience so much as the *traits* of experience. He speaks of the importance of how the states of experience grow character traits. What do experiences of being alive lead you to? connect you to? What character traits have the experiences grown in you?

Describe the feelings that have accompanied your experiences of feeling alive.

What can you do to increase the odds of having experiences?

Give some of those ideas a try and share your experiences at our next gathering.

Keep a journal this week. Record the first time this week that you watch the fog roll in or see the sun light up the pine or wash your face or break some bread. Then think about it and write out any discoveries or revelations. At our next gathering share something from your journal.

# EVENSONG

*Gathering Seven*

*Being Alive*

**Opening**

We gather here longing to feel more alive.
Our lives are exercises in longing.
Longing opens our eyes to glimpse
a holy presence, a radiance, a brilliance
at the heart of all creation.
Let us worship, and let us live with a Yes
on our lips and in our hearts.

right here,

**right now.**

Come, partake.

**Speak. Listen.**

ALL: Love boldly.

**Singing**

You are the great and fiery force,
In all alive, You are the source.
Shine through our eyes like stars above.
O, let our hands tell of your love.

**Reading from the
Common Bowl**

**Sitting in Stillness**

**Sharing Joys
and Sorrows**

**Remembering**

Our attentive listening to one another is a way to
show love and create the Beloved Community.

**Holding Each Other
in Silent Support**

**Communing**

Being Alive

**Responsive Reading**

Now you are ready—

**As ready as you are going to be.**

Neither you nor the world can wait for your
fears to subside.

**Step forward.**

You need no more preparation.

**You need no longer be on the outside observing.**

The world awaits not your timid hesitation,

**Not your clever critique,**

Not your tidy observations.

**The world invites your participation—**

**Singing**

"O Life That Maketh All Things New"
(Hymn #12 in *Singing the Living Tradition*)

**Giving Thanks**

**Closing**

Awaken your ears to the heartbeat of all
creation.
Open your eyes to the unexpected, the mystery,
the holy.
Embrace the ever present force,
moving through time and space,
holding you always in love.

## Readings for the Common Bowl

O world, I cannot hold thee close enough!

—*Edna St. Vincent Millay*

Surely the strange beauty of the world must somewhere rest on pure joy!     —*Louise Bogan*

Energy is the power that drives every human being. It is not lost by exertion but maintained by it.     —*Germaine Greer*

Life engenders life. Energy creates energy. It is by spending oneself that one becomes rich.     —*Sarah Bernhardt*

I postpone death by living, by suffering, by error, by risking, by giving, by losing.     —*Anais Nin*

The years seem to rush by now, and I think of death as a fast approaching end of a journey—double and treble reasons for loving as well as working while it is day.     —*George Eliot*

I was merely a disinterested spectator at the Banquet of Life.

—*Elaine Dundy*

People do not live nowadays—they get about ten percent out of life.     —*Isadora Duncan*

I had not loved enough. I'd been busy, busy, so busy, preparing for life, while life floated by me, quiet and swift as a regatta.

—*Lorene Cary*

Life was meant to be lived, and curiosity must be kept alive. One must never, for whatever reason, turn one's back on life.

—*Eleanor Roosevelt*

I like living. I have sometimes been wildly, despairingly, acutely miserable, racked with sorrow, but through it all I still know quite certainly that just to *be* alive is a grand thing.     —*Agatha Christie*

The most beautiful thing in the world is, precisely, the conjunction of learning and inspiration.     —*Wanda Landowska*

There are two ways of spreading light: to be
The candle or the mirror that reflects it.     —*Edith Wharton*

My least journey into the world would be a field trip, a series of happy recognitions.     —*Annie Dillard*

Earth's crammed with Heaven,
And every common bush afire with God.

—*Elizabeth Barrett Browning*

Grumbling is the death of love.     —*Marlene Dietrich*

Despite suffering, loss, and disappointment, life can be trusted.

—*Rachel Naomi Remen*

Some exciting things begin to happen when we dare to go beyond the stated boundaries in order to discover more of ourselves.     —*Sheila Collins*

We are able to laugh when we achieve detachment, if only for a moment.     —*May Sarton*

To me the pageant of seasons is a thrilling and unending drama, the action of which streams through my fingertips.

—*Helen Keller*

Birth is not one act; it is a process. The aim of life is to be fully born. To live is to be born every minute. —*Erich Fromm*

The life I want is a life of love and intensity, suffering and creation.

—*Walter Kaufmann*

. . . like holding to one's ear an egg that is due to hatch.

—*Doris Lessing*

Every morning is a cheerful invitation to make my life.

—*Henry David Thoreau*

The hills and the sea and the earth dance. The world of beings dances in laughter and tears. —*Kabir*

A world to be born under your footsteps. —*St. John Perse*

The dreamers have touched you. Sometimes you can look back over your shoulder and not pay attention. You can choose to be blind, or you can follow your destiny. —*Agnes Whistling Elk*

For occupation—this—the spreading wide my narrow hands to gather Paradise. —*Emily Dickinson*

I've set a task for myself . . . to cry and to laugh better and to create better and to love better. We have to feel our way for awhile and then suddenly we'll take a huge leap forward. We'll dare to name our emotions to one another. —*Ray Bradbury*

You had only to rise, lean from your window, and know that this indeed was the first real time of freedom and living, this was the first morning. —*Ray Bradbury*

We are the artificers of our own happiness.

—*Henry David Thoreau*

You can just relax, go with everything that's going, and praise God by liking what you like. —*Alice Walker*

Let us worship with our eyes and ears and fingertips; let us love the world through heart and mind and body.

—*Kenneth L. Patton*

This is a delicious evening, when the whole body is one sense, and imbibes delight through every pore. —*Henry David Thoreau*

Each second we live is a new and unique moment of the universe, a moment that never was before and never will be again.

—*Pablo Casals*

There is so much more to life than a perfectly clean kitchen floor.

—*Rachel Naomi Remen*

I look at the grass, the sky, the passersby, my companions, and my heart fills with a joy equal to any more obviously mystical or religious sentiment I have ever had. —*Peter Marin*

I want madness! I want to tremble, to be shaken, to yield to pulsation, to surrender to the rhythm of music and sea, to the seasons of ebb and flow, to the tidal surge of love. —*Sam Keen*

Come up with an expression (words, dance, art, song . . .) of your beliefs. Beliefs may change the next day or the next, but right now what are your beliefs?

What projects can you imagine this Evensong group taking on for this church? for the larger community?

How do you put or want to put your beliefs into action?

**Giving Thanks**

**Closing**

Keep alert, stand firm in your faith;
Be courageous, be strong.
Let all that you do be done in love.
*—1 Corinthians 16*

# EVENSONG

*Gathering Eight*

*Beliefs and Actions*

| Opening | Never doubt that a small group of thoughtful, committed citizens can change the world; indeed it's the only thing that ever has.<br>—Margaret Mead |

**Within the community, we discover gifts, abilities, and power that we did not realize we had.**

Within the community, we are emboldened and empowered to take stands and engage in struggles that we would not conceive of doing on our own.

**The faithful community experiences power rooted in love and resulting in justice.**

ALL: To be part of such a community is an honor and a powerful blessing.

—*Dennis A. Jacobsen, adapted*

| Singing | May we embrace all we can be.<br>May we each say Yes to ministry.<br>Each one is called and plays a part.<br>Fill us with power; our love impart. |

**Sharing Joys and Sorrows**

**Holding Each Other in Silent Support**

**Drawing One Another's Names from the Common Bowl**

**Sitting in Silence**

| Responsive Reading | We need the community to challenge us, |

*to encourage us,*

to summon forth our gifts,

**to fire our passion,**

to remind us of our calling.

**The community nurtures our discovery of the purpose and meaning of our lives.**

We need the community as well because we are battling principalities and powers, wickedness in high places.

**On our own we would be ineffectual, co-opted, or crushed.**

As a community, we experience a power that is greater than the sum of its parts.

| Remembering | Our attentive listening to one another is a way to show love and create the Beloved Community. |

| Communing | Beliefs and Actions |

| Covenanting | What action shall we take together?<br>How shall we continue? |

**Affirming**

| Singing | "We'll Build a Land"<br>(Hymn #121 in *Singing the Living Tradition*) |

# Response Form

Please take a few minutes before we close to write out some thoughts about our time together.

Name: _____

This Evensong series was . . . .

The best thing about it was . . . .

I wish we had . . . .

Something I'd change is . . . .

Another thing I'd like to say is . . . .

I came here wanting . . . .

I leave here . . . .

Overall, this experience was . . . .

Please include any additional comments or suggestions on the back of this page.

**Thank you very much for your participation.**